Daydreams in Mermaid Grass

by Natalie Williams

(JM)

JEREMY MILLS
PUBLISHING LIMITED

Published by Jeremy Mills Publishing Limited
www.jeremymillspublishing.co.uk

First Published 2008
Text © Natalie Williams

ISBN 978-1-906600-09-9

To my Mother, Jenni Williams,
who has shown me in her own life
the meaning and power of dreams.

Table of Contents

Foreword

This collection of poetry, *Daydreams in Mermaid Grass*, came to me for some unknown reason while travelling to work in Liverpool after a turbulent night of strange dreams. How often is it that we have the strangest visions, dreams, nightmares, ideas, deep thinking, imagined futures and saddened pasts visit us in the night?

I remember clearly once dreaming in black and white, a bright red rose leaping out into my mind's eye. How much can dreams touch us? At night, we are visited by the strangest views into unknown worlds where we may be Prince or Princess, raging dragons, slaying our enemies and victoriously riding home to our adoring friends and family.

Perhaps, at night, when all is resting and at peace, perhaps then we find those new worlds, when all we wish can become real, when all we truly feel and cannot say is spoken and what we cannot realise is played out for us in colour.

I introduce to you *Daydreams in Mermaid Grass*, a collection of tales, legends, stories, dreams and nightmares in poetry. I hope it transports you to places you have never been, shows you things you have never dreamt of or seen, and makes what seems out of grasp that little bit touchable.

Natalie Williams

Dactylion and Brontide

Dactylion, heart renderer and sweet love is lost.
He bore heart-rust his colours made,
and, rusted, his colours faded.
Sweetness lit his journey's walking,
travelled travelling, earth his apparels sundered,
thundered skies, lightning bared.

Dactylion, though sustenance did not sustain him,
pained he gained with each step
into mountains Tibetan and winding pathways.
His wrath for tides not in, subsided by nothing.
Angered with each tomorrow he saw,
each sorrow he bore.

Dust clouds his choking kissed.
Winds frosted his stroking face.
Air caught with death nemesis replace.
In his visions reverie he sore, he saw
Brontide's leaping.

Heart leaping, grim reaping.
Mirrored eyes shifted by glorious sight;
Brontide in pink flowers light.

Fair lilied Brontide's body of roses.
On his knees as his body left world and wonder,
his eyes stayed gazing
as death came glazing
over.

Il n'y a pas rien, pas rien.

Ravens Can't Sing

When I woke up this morning it was winter
And before it was spring
Robins are now ravens
Ravens can't sing
Dandelions painted daylight with gold
Now with ice and snow coloured cold

When I woke up this morning I was grey and unshaven
And what once was my haven
A place for misbehavin'
Now dribbled and stained
Muscles creeping and pained

When I woke up this morning in a long dream waking
As the dawn was breaking
I seemed to be taking
Too long or too shy
To be taking a leak
Now riddled and weak
As winter, relief seemed bleak

When I woke up this morning shivers had fogged up my portal
And I was suddenly struck
With the feeling of being mortal
And outside the red box of letters
Had been bound in fetters
Vandalised by bed-wetters
Happy kiddies with ice-creams
Now hoodlums with lost dreams

When I woke up this morning I realised I had been sleeping
And the sound that was creeping
Was it the sound of personal weeping?
Or that strange electric bleeping?

Ink in Evil Rain

Dance in this wicked rain
It's ink, watch it stain
Stain you with my pain
Aching, it's breaking
Set forth with this summer tide
And in words the storms hide

Spin in this evil rain
It's ink, watch it stain
Stain you, in hide and seek I've lain
Memories tossed, love is lost
Washed and squashed with acidity
Love is elusive, it's liquidity

Messy in this tortured rain
It's ink, watch it stain
Like Robin Hood with his merry men
Untrusting, unabided, this love's subsided
Run forth with abandon in this merry day
Wash your wicked feelings away

Boxed in this broken rain
It's ink, watch it stain
Using control once again
Mime at a window, these words a dildo
Bleed into the rain
Set your ink free, let it stain.

Come Away

Come away, young one, away from the dream
See the faces that peer to you from its stream
They call to you, do not answer a word
But fly away, fly away way little bird
Do not look upon them, their evil place
Will your love and heart with fear replace
Their torture, they are filled with dark and crows
They will tie you up with thorny bows
Come away, for your sorrow they know
And they cannot take you where you must go
Their quicksilver talons will rape your soul
Pour your love into themselves to be whole
So come away, young one, do not transgress
And life eternal with love I will bless.

Daydreams in Mermaid Grass

Daydreaming of daydreams
Of long forgotten yesterdays
Lollipops in Wonderland
Beavering a pool of mesmerized frozen spools in time
Jellies filled with ice cream
Shark infected, disease infested Mondays with buttons
for lunch hours
And pockets for break minutes
Cocaine cocktails
Slipping through the soul of Alice
And strike three, you're out

Daydreaming, daydreamed
Of all you never spoke of
And all you spoke you never meant
Highwaymen seducing gypsies
And strawberry milk
Skin so soft of silk
Pitted and fragmented
By sadness and tiredness and loveliness

Sinking by drinking
Blinking and all your lives are past
Why do you blink so fast?

Daydreams of cockles
With blue shadows
And sapphire moments
In an echo
Sunlight that only shines
In the darkest hours of night

Exposure to unimagined things
Silver linings?

At one with the sea
Bonded and flowing
Towards a new second of life
Of husband and wife
Son or daughter
And days like spinning wheels
Electric eels of feels
Demonstrated on the inside wall of your eyes
Like cinema picture reels

What dreams may come
When daydreams are long gone?
When all that can be dreamed is dreamt?
And all imagined is foreseen?
What will come to pass
Once ended daydreams in mermaid grass?

BirdMaster

"Trill, shrill', I call out, 'BirdMaster I once was'
And now I shout out to world unknown
Inside I am silent, though seem I so loud?
Ivory I am, the palest of skin
Eyes translucent, full of sin
I speak for no one hears
For this world I fear
Is lost to me, lost and unsung, like the silent passing of night'

'And I cry, cry, I weep to Falcon, I beg in fright,
'Falcon, my dreams are unspoken
I clutch a joy, so tight in my breast, my shroud
Of darkness, the shadows I play in
The light inside me so dim'
When Falcon calls
And from the skies he falls
I stay stuck, imprisoned and secluded; I am air, not the wind'

'And I am guilty, guilt it creeps, hurting thus, have I sinned?
Pain such as this, is it my love token?
Words jut out, I tear them from my mind
Peace such as I have dreamed, cannot find
When Falcon plays, and smiles to me
Feathered thus with power, such beauty
Oh Falcon, I cannot touch
You for you mean, vital to this world, too much'

'And then as my eyes peer out,
I slightly move for I have never seen such
Robin calls, to Falcon, she plays
Sweet little Robin, mesmerized I stare

And I cannot tear my eyes from there
Where she plays, with her eyes so fiery
And I am ivy overcome, entwined and overgrown
With fleeting love from Robin, Robin so red, shown'

'And as the memories play, while at my dreams I own
Raven laughs and cackles, but sweetly she breaks
Raven so true, but broken she is to me
Raven I wish to be
Peck me free, Raven call
Sing to me from your wishing well
While my wintry leaves they crack, and brown, and icily die'

'And Owl, Owl you there, hooting so dull, and laugh you cry
Uncovered, I see you
In my melting spring leaves
To my heart you try to cleave
It's night, it's day, but still you lie
In wait, and hungry you fly by
Torment me no more, for I cannot touch, though I feel so much.'

'And as I melt, I drip, I feel the watery jewels my heart touch
Hummingbird you buzz
You peck at Owl, oh the fuzz
Silly bird, you are so blue, sharp you are
And joyful I can hear you call from far
Various you seem, though various you are not
You try to pick at my death, my shame, my glorious decay'

'And beautiful he glides, into my heart abides,
Eagle you wish me away
Eyes you penetrate me, though I try to hide
And though I cannot run
You make me undone

While my flowers they try and bloom
I feel the impending doom
While I sing softly, Eagle becomes dim, and fades,
fade not into winged destruction'

'When I can smile no longer, and I feel no stronger,
Sparrow pecks at my confusion
And the sun shines on me
The bluest pearls of skylight dawn on my skin
And I feel the light shine inside me ... within?
My song becomes louder, until all can hear
And they listen in fear
And Hummingbird laughs in victory. Be ashamed you silly
bird, I gaily cry.'

'And I spin, I pass you by
The movement I feel,
Sets me off on a spinning wheel
Of pain, I swallow, I savor, I embrace
Until nothing left of myself I can trace
Don't touch me birds, my roses are in bloom
They may prick you, make you bleed, I need my room'

'And all you WingedOnes, you fly around my doom
I feel the lightest touch
For you I feel so much
I caress your hearts, your stares into my soul
For soon, soon my pretties I will be whole
I shake my roses, for their petals dark
And the change, I sing, open my mouth wide to hark'

'Birds, your master calls, I am the Lark
Drop from the sky; do fall
Touch my arms with your feathers of power

For I see, I saw your beauty; upon you I shower
My love, love's lost and love's gained
And with wings you touch me, for I shake my hair,
long and beauteous it seems'

'For you couldn't find, and I haunted your dreams
I am the Death-Bird, Dreamweaver
The bird of sickness, and fever
Of deception, and passion, and lies
To all seasons past ties
Mastered thus, I master you'

'Ride with me birds, of darkest fall you are due
For in the reddest autumn
Feel my tears, weepings of love
Drip to you from above
As I fly amongst you as BirdMaster
Let us fly my children, my loves, my wonders,
fly faster and faster.'

Faryla Dreamweaver

Faryla, dreams she is, dreams she can be
When she speaks, she speaks silently
With her eyes of glow
Love for life does show
Rise up wonders; do not sink low

Faryla alive, Faryla lost
Of earth's dust, heaven's wishes are her cost
With her skin so pale
Reddest hair in winter sails
And walk lively; all hearts do fail

Faryla Dreamweaver, Faryla truth believer
Love unfound, sweetness heart abound
And complete but wishing
Hoping, singing, and thinking
Searching yet not, Faryla's heart sinking

Of truth he speaks and journey he did
Steadfast and steady, he led
Riddles she bid
And to games she led
With all truth he did not gain
Faryla Dreamweaver's pain
For even with truth she found lie
And to heart that love deny

So to strength she bore
Faryla Dreamweaver she score
Prince of strength she couldn't find
A truth in his heart or mind

What wickedness her father wrought
When it was only love she sought
For even with strength she found him weak
And to adventure's future bleak

So to honour she did go
Palatable words and songs he did know
But with pain she bore
Honour gained no score
Faryla Dreamweaver, I do adore
With life of tears I feel your fears
And I have watched you all these years
At the very thought of you my heart sears

So with strength I speak
And with truth I'm meek
And with my words honour you
Faryla Dreamweaver, eyes so blue
Combined I am, sum of your dreams
You unloose me; tear at my seams
And I cannot hide from you
For you are all I seek, sought, all I am and do
And you kiss me it is true
What once was two is one, is one was two.

The Mockingbird and the Jewelfinder

I am ancient; I am old
So I sing, jewels to me bring
I am withered; I am cold, so cold ...
I shout out, let all the earth with my echo sing
Forced I am to this tortured call
Enter into my dusty, tattered hall
There you see drained and feigned
All the dainty jewels I have gained
But lost and died, I have lost their life
Lost their spark through my strife
So forced I am to shout and pray
For jewels I seek, jewels of night, jewels of day
Of the rainbow, of gold
Jewels of youth, jewels of old
So I may find the one that doesn't die
When I over its cold body sigh

Here I am, Jewelfinder
Mockingbird is my name; search is my game
I gain the sweetest stones
With immense and impressive speed
Pay me well with your sweet love
And I will bring you jewels, yea even from above
Fill me up with currency in kisses
And I will bring you the jewels of wishes
Jewels of promise, jewels of earth
Jewels of anger, and rage and rebirth
Jewels of torture, both hard and sweet
Jewels of love, both in victory and defeat

And you will find your jewel of fire
And you will laugh in power so dire

So you say, mockingbird
I will drink from the vial of your vow
So leave me now with this kiss
Take my love; take a bow
Slip from me, and hope you return
With the jewel of fire, the jewel of burn
To warm my soul now cold with fear
Cold, wasted, drowned in tears
There was once a time I could not cry
For tears into steam on me could pass by
Into the air they flew, leaving me as vapour
For fire I was and a fire that couldn't die
But I shall not speak of what passed
Of what happened in the last

So the mockingbird flew from me
To lands untold, unheard so speedily
Years they passed, ice I grew
Cold and colder is all I knew
I sang until I could sing no more
I sang the songs I had sung so many times before
Until my voice could no longer bear
The beg for jewels so I laid there
So Bird returned that night
With many jewels following in his flight

Dropping this, my Jewelfinder, you see?
I have brought many jewels to thee
Jewels of strange, jewels of pain
Jewels formed by the death of rain
Jewels of lightning in the sky

Jewels of where love has been passed by
Of a child's cry, or when a flower dies
Jewels of betrayal, and lows and highs
Jewels of denial, and urgency so true
Jewels of peace, and death I bring to you
Seek them through, the many they are
I brought them to you from afar

So I sifted with the last of my power
A jewel so sweet I see
Of a captured desert shower
Jewels of laughter, laughter for me
Jewels to tease, and to please
Jewels of endings, and beginnings
Jewels of silence and of singing
But when I got to the last
When my entire search had passed
And I lay back defeated
My search for fire beaten
Mockingbird, he did call out
He did scream, he did shout

'There! There!', he cried
'The jewel of fire it there abides
Look, oh Mistress, look again
The jewel of fire it does reign'
And so I glanced down to his stare
And saw the jewel of fire was there
Inside my body so cold and denied
The jewel of fire it had not died
Pulsing, pounding, it became strong
The more I stared; I stared long
Bloody and red, the jewel it bled
It bled red-hot fire as far as I could see

Until it began to envelope me
Warmed, I spun round and round
Until fire in my eyes it did abound
It caught the jewels sucked into my soul
All those jewels I knew made me whole
Part of me, they had been hiding
While in my prison I had been biding

The mockingbird, he laughed and played
He saw my fire and he obeyed

'Do not cast me aside O Ceaseless One
I will stay, warm me with your fire, I am undone
Let me singe my wings in your flame
So warm I may me, I may be the same
And so I spin, I let my fire free
So heated, beaten he could be
Until my fire it glowed around me
For the world; the earth to see.'

Mearl and Te'anara

She was part of the flowers, so proud she seemed
Her beauty a thousand men had dreamed
Dripping with dewdrops up on high
The golden sun and peerless sky
They filled with sweet enchantment her days
But her heart lay unfulfilled where she lay
Her skin, the palest hue of gold it glowed
As if the sun its very love had showed
And when she went this way and that
The birds ached for her, flew where she sat
Her dress was of ivy, ivory, and most ancient stones
Filled with the echoes of a man's thousand moans
Grew she did, and when he came,
Her heart stood still with weary pain

'Are you lost sweet Te'anara?' were words he said
'No fair seer, I am not lost,
merely wandering like the ant from its bed,
But where shall I find the sup to fill my loins
All I do is quarry and toil
It seems the Eden cannot give up its jewels to me
Or I am cursed, cursed more than another can be.'

'Sweet Te'anara, I will give you this seed,
It will guide you like a faithful steed
To where your fulfilment lies
And where you will forfeit all past ties
Where your journey ends, speak the name Mearl
And there you shall find your perfect pearl
But do no more than I permit
Do not bond to him where he sits

But bring him back to your dewed domain
Or the curse will come back again
For there you will stay made out of stone
And Mearl will tear his heart out with moan
For your curse will in part move to him
And he, in part, will fade to dim.'

And so the sweet Te'anara with her seed flew
Her heart sure of all she must do
And then she reached the whitest shores
Where the centaur Mearl hunts with mighty roars
She saw the frozen earth, so her heart tightened
Its beauty, its grace, she ached, bidden and brightened
And when she lay on the coldest domain
Her soul became one with the diamonds of the earth she gained

'Mearl, Mearl, come to me I seek
Let not my weary soul turn bleak
For I stand upon your frozen shores
And I hear the echo of your thousand roars
Let me fill your heart with my sweet caress
And to your heart, I kiss, I bless.'
And as she spoke, the earth it heard
And it gave up the centaur Mearl

His hair was like raw spun gold
As ancient as a dream weaver's fold
He echoed through the mountains so vast
Where he had roamed in play till night had passed
When the two came together
The snow peeled back where they stood seemed forever
Sweet Te'anara and Mearl they saw
Their love upon high where the snow its promise bore

And there sweet Te'anara sowed
Upon the flowers crushed and mixed with snow
Her seed of love for the centaur Mearl
For she had abandoned her promise of old
It grew and bore the sweetest flowers
And the sun wilted all the earth into showers
It gave up the seed of love
And called the seer from above
His mangled frame old from time
He threw his words down to the lovers in rhyme

'Te'anara, my life's jewel
How could you ruin, be so cruel
My toil has been laid to waste
Have you forgotten our bargain, with your love's taste?
Give to me your love's seed, oh earth
And I will give it sweet rebirth
If you return but to whence you came
And never return, no never again.'

'No, old seer these words I cannot hear
For the place of my seed is to be here
Where the winter's frost breathes pink to my cheeks
And my ivy tresses with their promise leak
Send me back if you cannot gain
The seed for yourself to relieve your pain
Return once more to my past lands
And make your mark again with your fair hands
For there is your true seed of love,
Not mine, old seer, not mine I say to you from above.'

The seer glimpsed in his very soul,
The ivy promise in her eyes of old
And sweet Te'anara he knew

His goddess fashioned from the morning dew
He left her there in the frozen shores
With Mearl she bore, whom she adores
And time passed on; each content
And the earth, it filled with promises kept and unkept
And there she slowly transformed into brown, the leaves so old
Her beauty gained from green to red,
and her ivy formed her ruby bed
And Mearl the hunter of the snow,
embraced her love forever more.

The Harbinger and the Jester

Twinkle twinkle shimmer his boots
In fun, in play are his roots
He growls like a bear, he makes play
Skip and trot he does along the path that day
'What whence I came, I laugh merrily,
Come red robin, hum away tweet tweetily
La-di-da, La-di-da fiddle may come
Feel my song become hum to the drum, drum'

Those were the words he sang on that road
In laughter, under sun, where no fear abode
His shoes were bells, they sang the sweetest tune
A story they told of love in the moon
And he spun, and twinkled and danced at play
As if his soul had wings that day
But darkness filled up, no matter his will
The sun went down, it had its fill

'Tra-la-la, Tra-la-la, come out sweet moon
Where you are, where you are, you shimmering buffoon?
I stamp my feet, I will twinkle my bell-bells
You must light my path for all to be well!'
So he sung that merry tune that jasmine night
Until the birds of day with joy took flight
They formed shapes of flowers, ribbons and bows
And he clapped and shouted with every pose

But the moon did not come out, nor light his path
She cowered in fear from the Harbinger's wrath
For the moon's beauty many a princess swore
The Harbinger, had whispered death afore

'Moon, do not light up, do not seek this prince
I will bleed you dry, until your suitors wince
I will seek him out, do not take flight
Let my eyes alone take up his sight.'

And so the Harbinger, red fire and fury
Set out that night as promised duly
Long her hair of centuries made
But that red fire's tresses could not fade
The air it reeked of the heat she bore
As if cowering in lava on a volcano floor
Black shadows she wore, her nipples of darkness
And her eyes broken promises of love and sweetness
She seemed as if to glide to the earth
Where the Jester played with merry and mirth
Until there she stood, bones dust her illusion
To bring the Jester's life to sweet conclusion
She raised her hand, as if at play
And breathed a breath of life away
And as she was about to set death free
She saw the Jester at the birds with glee

At his innocence and joy she felt her heart soften
Though fought she did at this sight
She watched him catch the robins at flight
His cheeks puffed out, his laughter booming
Until she could stand no longer to dooming
She turned in shame, and then saw her he did
He called out, ran behind an oak and hid
She stood frozen, breathless in fear unknown
And against herself, she slowly turned

'Come out sweet Jester, I mean you no ill.'
The world stood still.

'Harbinger I am, Harbinger I stay, Harbinger you see.
But please, continue with glee.'

He peeked, his face set in fear
But in her eyes he glimpsed a tear
And then against him, he rushed to her side
As if always there, he did abide
He blew onto her soft skin
The tear it flew onto the wind

'Harbinger, I am Jester so true
Do not be blue, fore say
I will at you giggle, hahaha away!'
And he glimpsed her soul that day

They stared thus eye into eye
And the birds whispered as they flew by
'What?!, Why?!, No!' they cried
In fun he lives, in death she abides
But skin to skin, the Jester and Harbinger as one
And in mirth she played
And in sadness he weighed
Tasted thus and mixed from two
One heart they filled, and the birds they did woo
They soared into heaven, and the earth they kissed
But their free souls they sorely missed
Until one day, they skipped as two
By day he fared, by night she dared
And in the twilight, they became one again bared

In twilight, they bore love and tore asunder
Until the world their passions admired in wonder
They became the raven, their love a jewel
They prayed for morn and night at bay so cruel

The moon held back as long she dared
And watched the lovers in their love-making fared
And so and so became their lives so true
Harbinger and Jester, in world of midnight blue

And the Jester sang these words of old
The bring warmth to those so cold
'Tra-la-la she fires me, I play, I sing
I fly upon her raven's wing
Of fire, of stone, of dust she's made
Forsooth I say, my love she bade
Formed and formed, form me I say
Tra-la-la, Tra-la-la come watch our day!'

And still the Moon can hear his song
Through all the night, as he sleeps along
And Harbinger does her work of old
Taking warmth to make it cold
Listen, young ones, you will hear them play
Seek out their stars, at night and at day

Nemesis

Nemesis you are, Nemesis away
Rooted you are in me, rooted you stay
Happy dreams we played, with sickness you stayed

Behind trees so ferny you hide and seek
In the forest of my forgotten mind
And with your wooded beauty gasping weak
Run to you, you so sweet I tried to find

And with jumping joy I jump, ha! Found you
And silent, ceased, erased, you aren't there
But smiling I hear you call, hear what you do
But when I get there, your lost place is bare

Sweetest angels they seem to follow me
Sweet Natalie, hear our sirenly calls
With jewelled promises your heart will fall

Lift me up into sweet, angelic dreams
And I am laughing, playing borne of fun
And smiling, grinning, I am torn undone

Seduce me, seducer, Nemesis mine
Nemesis so tortured, Nemesis fine
You so beautiful, mirage dressed in light
I see you shining to me in the night

And to the moon and sun and stars I shout
What are your mysteries, are you about
So beautiful to touch you run from me
Expelled by me, repelled, set free by me

Drunk intoxicating distant wonder
You are memory, memorised so asunder
Pink of sunny flowers so simple and true

I gaze about me in your happy mind
What beauteous Nemesis I there find
And in the morning your sunrise it shines
You pass me by; around me draw your lines

I am spinning, I turn to stare, to look
Kitten in wool, you write me in a book
And I feel the heat of you; make me burn

Nemesis, you are made of thorny fire
Of you it seems I cannot run or tire
Nemesis, don't you know, why do you go?

Why do you destroy what you love?
I send for help with my white turtledove
'Nemesis, no! Don't set me alight
Set alight, I came to you in the night

Nemesis, no!' I cry, do not make me die!
Come let's, let's just play hide and seek
You can laugh; laughing you can make me weak
again; but destroy me, destroyed you do
Destroy me as comes natural to you
I am a book and you are immortal fire
This nightmare, oh God, it seems so dire

Nemesis, Nemesis I am burning
My stomach aches, my stomach turning
And into your eyes I look, eyes I look
Why did you burn me, burn your pretty book?

Nemesis, Nemesis I am dying

And to you I smile, to you beguile
And you hold out your hand, get up you stand
And while I am crying, while I'm crying
You leave me a while; you leave me a while

Nemesis, our fingers just touched the tips
But water you do not give me in sips
Nemesis now I see, Nemesis I see
In a dream, so dreamy of you and me

Imagined you were, and I am destroyed
And this mortal game we played, just toyed

Nemesis now I see, Nemesis I see
In the pool of reality, ashes dust
See your face and I must die, dying must be
Separate from you, separate I must
What once, what once was book is now all dust
Is now all dust.

Gaelic Eyes

You are beauty. She is beauty.
Gaelic eyes
That compose a song
Enough to pull you along

Gaelic eyes
Multicoloured dream coat
Melting into buttery high and low notes
In a boat 'I love you' letters float

Gaelic eyes
Too beautiful to touch
Too lonely to clutch
Filled with quavers and half moons of green
I owe you so much

Gaelic eyes
Eyes of wonder
Communicate to me in extended sound
Gaelic eyes, disbelieving I've found

Gaelic eyes
Filling universes and plateaus of skies
Tell you where you've been
All you can become
All you have seen
Wrapped in symphony
Composed in liquid fluidity
Gaelic eyes, looking back at me.

As The Crow Flies

As the crow flies
Let go of past ties
Stop in cessation the lies
Forget all you remember
Let pain be removed from you
DISMEMBER
Set free all connection
And so set free the distention
Look up at the skies
As that crow flies
In a moment
In a memory
Let this be your minute
Your seconds of reverie
Leave behind
ORDINARY
Kill the unusual
And let the crow form the new visual
Dove black roses
And Monday morning poses
Of kisses stole in darkness
Languor languishing
Outlined in naked glory
DISTINGUISHING
Fall backwards
Forwards
Sideways
Into love highways
Be all you are
And let your crow fly so far
Black as acid tar

Burn your mark into the forehead of time
Push with your finger
To those disrespectful hard days
And say BRING IT ON
Sideways!
Let loose
On normal unsuspecting life
Catch it unsuspecting
And watch the diamond studded memories
In the eyes of your crow
Reflecting

Leopard Lover

Leopard lover
With a roar your recover
What was lost and could not be found
With an ivy crown of serpentine
Onyx dreams
You raise your colors
From the ground
With streams
In a catlike and grotesque pose
Angry and tortured
Terrible your skin
All you are is visible to me
From right
Within
Step out your spots
Tail wrapped
While I napped
Round my throat so seductive
Yet destructive
Leopard lean, leopard loving
I am undone
And cannot awaken
Let my strange love for you not be forsaken

Lady in the Looking Glass

Your eyes are so ken
Weighed down by shades of green
And all you've seen
As you phase out of today
You become a dream
Magnetic and eclectic
Eclipsed by tomorrow
With all your faded wishes of tomorrow
You weep of sadness of love untrue
Your eyes weighed down by shades
Of blue
Disappeared what once you revered
With age now seared
With the melancholy of birds
That fly in your reflection
Ribbon ships set sail
Discoveries of doomsdays and Tuesdays
When all your unspoken prayers break into song
Lady
You sit and gaze
At your looking glass too long …

Wishing Well of Tomorrow

One (plops)
Just one (plops)
Into the waters
Still and lidless
Tormenting, tormented I gaze
Until my lids glaze over
Into the wishing well of tomorrow
I pour my melodies and scribbles

Two (plops)
Just two (drops)
And not the tears of strength or laughter
But of expectancy
And so I stand
With a hand emptied
Searching for a moving script
Of a mummy from a crypt
He tears his bonds and I still
Stand
Amazed …

A Griffin's Tale

Destiny, destined destining
In an eggshell a griffin lying
With mottles of bottles of liquid tragedy
Satan's circle of never ended progeny
Thorn tiara with a bubble of mass destruction
Evolving, gold circlet of sexual compulsion

Skin of soft silk
Sheerly bleeding love milk
Tyrannized by perfection
Liquids metallic spill
What Gods have willed
Needs must not be killed
Not shattered
Not gloomed
Too magnetic
And chromed to be doomed

Fatalistic fantastic
So pathetic drastic
Little Griffin lay
As sun rose in heat
Exposed he lay dying

Quicksilver

Pray for death
Pray for ravens dipped in quicksilver laced with shadow avengers
Pray for spicy things
Pray sagacity and emblem brings
Feign solitude and end to umbral adventure
Give way to dementia

Seek peace and pursue it
Lead cease and imbue it
Quicksilver
Just a sliver
Just a touch
All is not forgotten
All is not lost
Bodice up dreams
Cry wolf twice thrice
Count the cost
Blot out colours weaved out motion
Quicksilver
Potion
Remember in your eyes
All you saw was unseen
Wake up
'Tis a quicksilver dream

Natalie Williams

Geisha Girl

You are a star
Four pointed and not quite perfection
I make wishes on your lips
Millions of inconsequential wishes

While you are sleeping
The moon and sky cry weeping
I clutch at all the thousands of dreams I have
I believe I am dreaming
Your presence melts shattered tomorrows
All I am is my gift to you
Daisied eyes, damson dressing
Belief in this vision of you is my blessing

Gaze into my sleepy time, Geisha Girl
As I trip into midnight.

Pendulum

Pendulum, I start to swim
Not forgetting all the things I learnt
The clock is ticking
And I can't stop this sinking
Grandfather clock of old
It seems mother's pie has gone so very cold
Brother's so bold
He grabs a slice
But it's cold as ice
In the heat of that summer afternoon
My eyelids drooping
Eager beaver
But they awaken
From the glint of Grandmother's cleaver
Silver
Mother's shouts ring down the hallway
'That pie was for Sunday!'
And I smile through treading sleep
While the dog in his cot seems to groan and weep
Catching flies with his teeth
The sound of muffled pages turning
And the roaring fire
With coals burning
Drift me away, like 'Tag, you're it!'
While in Grandpa's armchair I sit
The smell of pies and sweet cigars
Drift into my summer daydreams
I've found my warming place
Where the sun hits my face
And the gold light streams
The dog is chasing

It's a merry tale
What seems to me like a jug of ale
I yawn and ponder
He yells of fright
Suddenly I realise it's turned to night
The smell of toast on the warm evening wind
It seems the day's toils
Like a pool's been skimmed
Marmalade kisses warm their breath on my cheek
'Tomorrow begins a new week'
They say, kiss my sleepiness away
Wake up ... Wake up ... Wake up
Pendulum, I cease to swim.

Mistress Red Hair

Red haired, red headed mistress, wanderer
In lilac flowers and bloody showers, coverer
Oat fields are your promise, curves oh lusty
And in bat engaged caves so musty
Fusty, you walk in shrouded black
Walking forwards, reverse back
Slow, transfixed by memories, red hair
You walk to then, and back and there
Walk to whom, and walk to show
Walk to lose your life, walk to grow
And naked your promise, nipples so fair
You are seemly, mistress red hair.

Dragon Dust

Mi Amore, I am red
Tinker with me, collect and sustain me
Feel your flight graze me, it pains me
I am red in the eye
And red in the wing
And red when I sing
Your memories I abuse
I will thoroughly use
All the words in worldly life to gain me
Scales form the drops of love I have grown
Snake-like eyes, so horrible true form seeds I've sown
I seem so terrible, but how unjust
These words you spin break apart I must
I am soft yonder, on you I ponder
Bronze of light, bronze-like flight
You tease me with your teasing eyes
And time you take from me, you guard
From all unsavory days you're barred
Keep me close. Keep me from end
And all your sadness and child-like tears I'll mend.

Angels' Rhapsody

Torturous, incestuous, these words I utter
Hungry, insatiable, unsatisfied I mutter
For your words I yearn, and touch I burn
I ache and plead for you my heart bleeds
And I seem so childlike, so immature
While you seem so wise, so seemly, so pure
Innocent, and unfulfilled I am, I speak
To you but you are too weak
Caress me, cuddle me, cajole me
Look into my crying eyes and see
Dying eyes, dying for you
Sickness takes me, what does it do
I cannot separate me from you
For we were once two
But one we are, near now not far
Sealed my love for you in a jar
I seem so cold, and yet so heated
For your love my stubbornness has berated
Why do you seek me, weak me, peak me
Sing to me with the songs of angel's rhapsody
When I lie awake at night
Lie in the black, the shadows time, the lack of light
I close my eyes, see you looking, staring, gazing
Coy warrior, and I laugh so softly
You touch me so tenderly
And intake of breath, so silent I seep
For your skin on mine burns me in my sleep
Time stops, lips on my body, so torn I seem
Are you real, or just a dream?
For you once were lost, are you found?
These memories, these thoughts, abound

So close, feel the heat, your heartbeat
Stinging the tears in my eyes, my defeat
I give in, I submit, I reach into, closer to you
And I sleep, I dream, so sweet, do what you do.

Nightmare Angel

Wings held on by wax
Let fly like cotton flax

Eyes of emerald babies smitten
Read ancient scribbles of bibles unwritten

Limbs of limbered gold
Mere mortals, riches unjust and undiscovered

Studded with heartbreaks and suicide blisses
Breathe forth to me with graveyard kisses

Graveyard Kisses

Graveyard kisses
And near misses
With a hint of mint
Just a glint of light
Glued shut
With promises unborn
Loneliness fires forth
In that dark cold shatter
What does it matter?

The Sorceress
and the Pocketpicker

Tick tock, pick your lock
Pickerpocket never stop
Be fortress, be castle, I make a mock
Relieved of jewels and crowns ye'll be
Picked clean ye'll see lock and stock

Shining jewels encrusted, weaved into majesty
I cannot find, not potion speak
What dreams may come
Or shadows unfold
When all leaves this world in cover cold

Ellipse gardens of midnight
Spotlight
Out of phantom flickers
Friend with friend bickers
Cat evolutes to dragon
Raven disappears into tomorrow

Transformed from purity into wickedness
Bathed in diamond secrets
Sorceress walks in promise
Floats poised in stardust

In market green goblins' fluids whittled and strained
She unwittingly obtained
Whistle magical and unjust
A whistle of tomorrow's lust
Bonnysooth, the pirate heard her ringing

As if a siren singing
The burly pirate magically transported
To her castle stony ivory cast

Though summer's day had chanted
Sorceress, she, cursed lay love departed
Bonnysooth bore her into safer times
Where peace is written into rhymes

And so she blew hard her whistle
Creamed her face with milk thistle
Beautied love she whistled at half past seven
And he reverted to sea at half past eleven

Months of this sweet cherry passed by
Until Pocketpicker in dark of night
Stole the whistle in leather tights
She thereupon discovering
Her murderous rage let loose
She swore to take the thief's entrails
And let him hang upon a noose

Pocketpicker journeyed far
Seeking jewels and trinkets in lands unknown
Bearing gold and treasures
Sick with sadness Bonnysooth wreaked vengeance without
measures
He plundered sailboat and tailcoat
Sinking all in his path
The world had never seen such wrath
But Sorceress was maddened and saddened
Bonnysooth had not spoken
What in his heart she'd awoken

And in his terrors unsubsided
Pocketpicker's ship with blood divided
Sinking down to land and graveyard
Whistle bound in tears
The world passed by in its infancy
Grew old and toothless in its years
Bonnysooth and she
Separated indefinitely.

Words of Cursing

So you could not speak
You'll stay unspoken
All you wished and wet upon shall due broken
All you loved shall be stood upon
Slowed in twists of hate
This, my young, sprite your fate
Until you seek out and lay open
All that you've unspoken
My curse on your skin
Shall drive you muttering, muffled and dim
Until you lit loose as I bid
What you hid from your inside within.

The Curse of Love's True Soldier

Drink from my golden malice
Spit love to me in my tainted chalice
Painted with lyrical splendour
Defend to me, defender
Long to smear your desire a little higher in a line on my leg
Peg your hoping to my groping
Wish for eloping
Tear your list for me into rusted dust
Spell out my name with links from a spider web
Be vigilant
With your pursuance
Let no barrier be hindrance
Drip-feed me into your mould of perfection
Like a confection
Metallic liquid silver
Glitter gaunt with specks of immoral immortality
Your lust for me
It speaks unjust
For I am love's true soldier
Be bolder.

Bracken Forest

Dark gnarly shoots in Bracken Forest grew
Long of old
With depressive and repressive
They timed forth into the cold
What once was glee and fulfilment laid
Filled with sorrow on the morrow glade

There lay a small undiscovered things
Nor speak
Nor spoken
Nor everything
Pretty, gaudy shining wings
Bent out of frame
Speaker was its name

Speaker spoken, nay untrue
Speaker never spoke
For he was of dew
And of leaves
And evening eves
Hair of golden light
Highlighted with deepest darkest night
Speckled with broken promises
Abusive were his eyes of shadow
Dove's eggs that never hatched
Cursed he was.
The Speaker who could not speak.

Words he could not find
Until he murmured
Out all things in his mind

The sounds that leaked from his beak
Were weakness weak
Phosphorous and of jewels cracked
True words Speaker lacked

He bled
Until all blood had fled
And he lay blue and cold
Right there in Bracken Forest so old.

Natalie Williams

Komodo Princess

Breathe life into thee
Sounds of Hawthorne
Lilied kisses
Leaves of skin with ruby coral softness
Entering me within
Pepper tongue with spice of nice
Of taste and wine
Princess, feeder
Komodo beleaguered and combined
Komodo Princess you see
Komodo Queen you'll find
Dress of scales
Bloomed of cat's eye
And frequented
Sewn together by evils demented
Stitched into hearts

Filled into eyes
Propped into eyes
'How fare thee Speaker
Hearken thee sweet blessed one
Hay of mirrors and apples of seeds
Why doth thee bleeds?
I am reversed
Painted onto the backside of time
Blurted forth into wickedness
Into your moment of death
How sublime.

I make love to your leaving life
I become wife to thee

Bee of death I am
Bee my honey

Speaker, speak or I shall laugh at thee
Speak as you are
Speak blank verse afar
Nay speak monotone monotonously
Take my satin elliptically
Nippled coffins
I bear for thee
Words of curses and all thee cherish
More love for thee thy will endure
I shall bleed into you thy cure

A dozen lives formed Speaker
For of things he was, of things he became
A dozen ferocities formed his viscosities
Misery and sickness
Victims of yesterday
That trip to tomorrow
So he was formed of sorrow

Of challenge
Of survived stormy madness
Speaker spoke

Natalie Williams

The Crow and the Mirror Dragon

The Crow and the Mirror Dragon
Set out one day
Though they travelled in fours
Now in pairs
So as not to give the game away

Flew over fields of ribbons
Daffodils of glass
In the grass
Painted into landscape
With glitter
So they bordered up above in the skies

Crow was midnight and ungainly
Though he spoke plainly
He uttered in mutters
Ancient text in flutters
Scribbles murmured by sound
And he had not touched the ground

Dragon, though older not wiser
Vainer, a disguiser
Bore fractures of fractions
All who had seen him
And memories and senses of all who had been him

Though unlikely a pair
Black and mirror in sun glare
Sky baby blue and unfrequented

With their twosome dented
They fell into poppies red ablaze
Trapped in summers gaze
Mirrored crow dreams in a maze
Who could have foreseen

Scales of painted starlight
And black as shadows born
They tore at each other
Malice, hatred and scorn
Until seeping, tired laying
Their actions weighing
In confusion solely nurtured
They philosophised and harboured

So they grew mossy and ferns breaking
With wings upward waking
Leaving maze taking
Wisdom gained, wisdoms spreading
To Bracken Forest they flew heading

Seeking tales of shimmered darkness
They wore into midnight
Tearing unearthly vision into sky
Crow and Mirror Dragon flew by.

Speckled Dragon

Siva
Shiver
Speckled Dragon
Born electric
Come what may
Drink fire in china
teacups

Exhumed and eely
Lemon fucking squeezy
Cannabis delights sum up
his equation
To honour borne
His inflation

Siva
Quiver
Jelly are my knees
and I say
Oh my
Speckled Dragon please
Pubescent are my dreams
of speckled dragons on speed.

Whore in a Crypt

Tight jeans and bottled dreams,
dreams like fake tan.
Earrings in brown illusion,
an end without plan.
Mirrored into submission ...
Fake eyelashes tinted, glinted and flinted
by nuclearotic fission.
Casual Fridays into weekdays and weekends.
Forgivings takes place,
turning to apologetic amends.
Losing friends into strangers.
Swopping adventure for dangers.
Desserts into deserts,
whore in a crypt.

About the Author

Natalie Williams was born in 1981 of African-Irish descent, in the newly formed country of Zimbabwe on the purple carpeted Jacaranda Lane. Life was filled in her early years with Irish fairy tales written by her grandfather, and the inspirational imaginings of the world of Narnia and Grimms' Fairy Tales. In the inspiring world of Africa, she began her journey as a writer, winning an Honours award for her poem 'The Thicket and the Musgrove' at the age of nine. Years later, she now launches her first poetry collection, drawing on the inspirations of her life and imagination.

www.natalie-williams.com